Big Little Book on Ansible Automation

Contents

Big Little Book on Ansible Automation **1**

Introduction **5**

What is Network Automation? **6**

    Provisioning vs Configuration Management **6**

What Is Ansible? **7**

    Idempotence **7**

    Installing Ansible on Debian and Centos **8**

    Running Ansible **8**

YAML File Structure **11**

Ansible Folder and File Structures **13**

    Top-level Folder Structure **13**

    Role Folder Structure **14**

    Role Setup **14**

    Using Roles in a Playbook **14**

    Role Locations **15**

    Role Files **15**

Ansible Galaxy **17**

    Role Scaffolding **18**

    Roles from a Requirements File **18**

    Galaxy Commands **19**

Structure of Ansible Playbooks **20**

    Playbook Components **20**

    Play **20**

    Task **21**

    Inventory **21**

    Module **22**

    Role **22**

Running Playbooks **23**

    Playbook Example **23**

Inventory Setup **26**

Variable Precedence **28**

Sequencing Playbooks in Ansible **29**

Handlers **29**

Nested Includes **29**

Using Conditions in Ansible **31**

Waitfor Condition **31**

Ansible Vault **33**

What Is Ansible Tower? **34**

Installing Tower **34**

Navigating Ansible Tower **35**

A Note About Permissions **36**

Projects **36**

Inventories **36**

Templates **37**

Job Templates **38**

Workflow Job Templates **38**

Menu Settings **39**

Credentials **39**

Current User **40**

Settings **40**

Roles **42**

API **43**

Tower-cli **43**

My View **45**

View Documentation **45**

Logout **45**

Conclusion **46**

Introduction

Hi there and welcome to the Big Little Book on Ansible Automation. This book was written with both the new IT recruit and the seasoned IT professional in mind, but with a view to aid fast recall of information without having to lift a four-hundred-page tome!

As well as condensing detailed technical facts, it is accompanied with useful hints to help the concepts and understanding of the ideas stand out. Handy for those work or interview situations where there's just not enough time to filter out the pertinent information from all that text.

Take care and happy reading.

U V Omos

What is Network Automation?

This is the utilisation of programming/coding and provisioning platforms to build networks and infrastructure without the need for human intervention. It mainly removes the need to manually carry out repetitive tasks, letting computers do the work instead.

This book focuses on the use of programming and tools to automate the provisioning and configuration management of devices.

Provisioning vs Configuration Management

Provisioning is the creation and implementation of resources. But that is where it stops. If a service has been provisioned and then needs changing, a provisioning tool will simply destroy the current service and create it again.

A configuration management tool also creates and implements resources. But if these resources need changes, a configuration management tool doesn't destroy the resource but instead modifies its current state so that its new state fits the stipulated requirement.

This book will look at Ansible as a *configuration management* tool.

Let's crack on with looking at Ansible.

What Is Ansible?

Ansible is a configuration management tool that can be used to deploy multiple device types from implementation all the way to on-going management and maintenance. Red Hat created Ansible as a configuration management tool with template facilities and a declarative configuration file syntax making it straightforward to use for various types of network and platform engineers.

It uses pre-configured tasks to carry out changes on network devices, with each task running a command or a set of commands to achieve its aim.

Idempotence

Ansible works on the basis of idempotence, which means that it aims to achieve a consistent state for all of the devices it configures. For example, if a device's target software version in a playbook is 10.1 it will always target this as the definitive version during the running of this playbook. Therefore, if the current version is 10.0, Ansible will upgrade it. After this initial upgrade, Ansible will ignore any playbook tasks requesting an upgrade. Take note of the following modules as these are the main modules currently used often by engineers that are not idempotent.

- Shell
- Command

Installing Ansible on Debian and Centos

We have used an Ansible installation on the Debian operating system throughout this book. The only prerequisite is Python.

Using a platform of your choice which already has Debian installed on it, use the following commands to install Ansible on the local device.

```
sudo easy_install pip
sudo pip install ansible
```

Currently installation instructions can be found for all operating systems at the following link.

https://docs.ansible.com/ansible/latest/installation_guide/intro_installation.html

Running Ansible

This can be done using the following executables.

- Ansible executable
- Ansible-playbook executable

These are described further below.

Ansible executable

This entails executing a command directly on the required device using command line arguments. For example, an Ansible ping (different from an ICMP ping) can be executed on 192.168.1.1 using the following syntax.

```
ansible -m ping 192.168.1.1
```

The –m switch (module switch) calls the ping module, which runs on the required devices and yields output similar to the following.

Ansible-playbook executable

This entails executing a set of arguments specific to a device based a YAML (Yet Another Markup Language) configuration file known as a playbook and on its entry in an inventory file. The inventory would contain device specific information such as IP address or hostname and credentials amongst other items. Further arguments can also be supplied using the –e command line switch (these arguments would have precedence over those in the inventory file).

```
ansible-playbook -i inventory.txt
getversion.yml
```

The following is an explanation of what this example is actually doing. The -i switch (inventory switch) refers to the actual inventory (device list) that the command will run against. An inventory is simply a list of devices that the ansible-playbook command will interrogate using the specified playbook. It is quite similar to a device hosts file. The inventory file can be called anything as shown in the following example.

```
ansible-playbook -i list getversion.yml
```

getversion.yml this is the playbook containing the set of tasks that will be launched on the target machines listed in the inventory called 'list'.

That's all that is needed to run a playbook. Further switches are available and options can be added using the –e switch but more on this later.

There are a number of other options for specifying arguments and their order of precedence will be shown later on in this book as will the running of playbooks. This book focuses on running Ansible using playbooks instead of the command line so will use the ansible-playbook command.

YAML File Structure

As stated in the previous section, Ansible uses YAML files to store its declarative syntax in text format. The typical file structure is shown below.

```
---
- hosts: all
  roles:
    - role_name
```

A Brief Note on YAML. YAML stands for Yet Another Markup Language and its syntax follows a 'declarative' programming model (they simply tell you the end state required) as opposed to an 'imperative' programming model which tells you how to go about reaching an end state).

Note that YAML files use indented spaces and not tabs. So, each indent is actually two spaces.

Now let's go back to putting together a playbook using YAML and the YAML syntax.

Each folder would have a main.yml file containing the top-level syntax used to build and configure the relevant devices.

The following is an example of a playbook used to install Node.js on a server is shown below.

```
---
dependencies: []

---
```

```yaml
- name: Install Node.js
  yum: name=npm state=present enablerepo=epel

- name: Install forever module to run Node.js
  nom: name=forever global=yes state=present

- name: Install npm modules required by app
  nom: name={{ item }} global=yes
state=present
  with_items: "{{ node_npm_modules }}"

#Add the node_npm_modules variables

node_npm_modules:
  - forever
  - async
  - request
```

Define the meta information in this file. This describes the role to Ansible and Ansible Galaxy (more on this later).

Ansible Folder and File Structures

Before continuing this section, it is worth noting that a playbook doesn't actually need the folder structure described in the following sections to run. This structure is mainly used to avoid repetition of folders in a directory structure. For instance, if there are two playbooks called switch.yml and router.yml which both need to run another playbook snmp.yml but the switch.yml and router.yml playbooks are kept in different directory locations, then it is worth considering a folder scafolding structure to house the snmp.yml playbook in a 'network management' role.

Top-level Folder Structure

The main folders that can be configured are as follows.

app/
roles/
 role_name/ (contains main.yml)
  meta/
  tasks/
  handlers/

Ansible uses and has a library of online roles that can be used for building and deploying configurations.

Role Folder Structure

The structure of a role's folder is typically similar to that shown below.

role_ name/
  meta/ (contains main.yml)
  tasks/
  handlers/

Role Setup

You would typically have your main playbook in the root of the folder. Then this folder would have a folder called roles that would contain all of the Ansible roles. This roles folder would then have a subfolder representing each role, e.g. cisco. This cisco folder would then have subfolders for each of the role's components. These component folders would be as follows.

default, files, handlers, meta, tasks, templates, vars

Ansible requires the folders to be named exactly as shown above for the role to work correctly.,

Using Roles in a Playbook

The following shows how to connect a role to a playbook
running – this example shows how to connect the
Juniper.junos role.

```
---
- name: Check Firewalls
  hosts: firewalls
  roles:
    - Juniper.junos
```

Role Locations

Roles can be saved in the default path shown below.

```
/deploy/ansible/roles:
/deploy/ansible/community/roles
```

If not, the roles can be configured in the ansible.cfg file using
the role_paths setting.

```
roles_path=/gcl/juniper/roles:/gcl/cisco/roles
```

Note that a role's folder can be named anything e.g. standard,
network

but it helps to make it a meaningful name for clarity,
especially if multiple users are running playbooks.

Role Files

This section shows a typical role setup. It will use the following folders/files.

- File: meta/main.yml
- File: files/default.conf
- File tasks/copy.yml
- File files/index.html
- File: handlers/main.yml

As mentioned previously the main folders required by a role are meta, tasks and handlers. The files folder is provided just as a location to save the default.config and index.html files and is not required for a role setup as standard.

The contents of each file are shown below.

File: meta/main.yml

```
---
dependencies
   {role: base}
   include: copy.yml
```

File: files/default.conf

This file is getting copied to the server as part of a yml task.

```
server{
   listen 80;
   server_name localhost;
}
```

File files/index.html

This is a standard html home page file.

```
<html><head><body><p>This is a standard html
home page file.</p></body></head></html>
```

File tasks/copy.yml

This file copies the early configured default.conf and index.html files to the web server.

```
---
- name: copy
  copy:   src=default.conf
dst=/var/www/html/default.conf
  copy:   src=index.html
dst=/var/www/html/index.html
```

File: handlers/main.yml

This file restarts the apache service after a relevant configuration has been made such as the change of the http port used by the server from the standard http port to a bespoke port.

```
---
- name: restart apache
  service: name=apache state=restarted
```

Running the playbook in the app folder combines these actions with the net effect of deploying all of the commands in the playbooks.

Ansible Galaxy

This is the online repository for open source developed roles that can be downloaded and used in your local Ansible deployments.

You can download and review previously prepared roles from it using the following command.

```
ansible-galaxy install cisco.router
juniper.firewall
```

This would install the Cisco router and Juniper firewall roles to the local machine.

Role Scaffolding

This is a means of building and download roles from Ansible Galaxy. This is out of scope for this book but there is a considerable amount of information on role scaffolding on the Ansible Galaxy website located at https://galaxy.ansible.com.

Roles from a Requirements File

Roles can also be installed by using a YAML file e.g. requirements.yml. The syntax of this file would be as follows.

```
- src: cisco.router
- src: juniper.firewall
```

This could be called from the command line as follows.

```
ansible-galaxy install -r requirements.yml
```

These roles could then be used to deploy a Cisco router and a
Juniper firewall in a playbook as follows.

```
---
- hosts: all
  become: yes

  roles:
  - cisco.,router
  - juniper.firewall
```

Galaxy Commands

Key commands are as follows.

```
ansible-galaxy install - install role
ansible-galaxy list - list the currently
installed roles
ansible-galaxy remove - remove an installed
role
ansible-galaxy init - initialise a role for
uploading to Galaxy
```

Structure of Ansible Playbooks

Playbook Components

The main components required for launching and Ansible playbook are shown below.

- Play: referenced in the actual playbook file
- Task: referenced in the actual playbook file
- Inventory: referenced at the command line
- Module: referenced at the command line

Optional components are shown below.

- Role: referenced in the actual playbook file

These are described further below.

Play

A play is a single executable set of tasks required in order to achieve the playbook's requirements. It is the sum total effect of the playbook's commands. This is the top-level component of a playbook and all of its tasks run on a single device or a common group of devices. For instance, if a command can be run on the entire estate then the play can be configured to run on all devices with the 'hosts: all' setting in the inventory. But if it can only run on www servers in the inventory (explained later) then it won't run correctly on any other devices and will cause the playbook to show output stating that it did not complete correctly. A playbook can have multiple plays e.g. the first play could be on web servers, the second on database servers and so on.

Task

A task is a single item from the play that achieves one of the play's requirements. A number of tasks could be needed to complete a play.

Inventory

This is the list of one or more devices that the play is executed on.

Module

This is a set of commands particular to a device or technology that can be included in a play. For example, it could be a Cisco or Linux command module. A module must be declared in the playbook so it knows where to look for the commands it has to run. Ansible is installed with a set of current modules written for different operating systems and devices, from Cisco to Linux and these abstract the functions they launch from the user taking away the need for imperative function writing in favour of declarative syntax. In other words, modules help the playbook author focus on the what instead of the how. The location of the list of modues at the time of writing can be found at
https://docs.ansible.com/ansible/latest/modules/list_of_all_modules.html.

It is also possible to write your own modules and instructions for this can be found at
https://docs.ansible.com/ansible/latest/modules/developing_modules.html.

Role

A role is a set of characteristics built in order for Ansible to carry out its commands on a particular make/model of device e.g. Cisco or Linux. It is the representation of a device type in folders that can be referenced by playbooks in order to carry out commands on the devices relevant to it.

Running Playbooks

Playbooks must be configured in YAML files as shown earlier. Each playbook must have the following.

- Inventory
- Credentials

These can be configured for each playbook in its scaffolding or supplied at the command line with the following command line switches

- –i for the inventory file
- –e for the credential settings

Playbook Example

For example, the following will run a playbook with the inventory.txt inventory file and credentials of admin and password for the user and password.

```
ansible-playbook showconfig.yml -i
inventory.txt -e "username"
```

The playbook shows the configuration of a Juniper device using a previously installed juniper.junos role is shown below.

```
---
- name: Check Firewalls
  hosts: firewalls
```

```
roles:
  - Juniper.junos
connection: local
gather_facts: no

tasks:
  - name: Check Cxn
    wait_for:
      host: 192.168.1.1
      port: 22
      timeout: 5

  - name: Show Config
    juniper_junos_command:
      host: 192.168.1.1
      user: admin
      passwd: password
      port: 22
      commands:
        - "show configuration"
    register: response

  - name: "Print result"
    debug:
      var: response
```

The earlier described components are found as follows this playbook example.

- Play: the playbook in its entirety
- Inventory: all the devices in the **hosts** section of the linked inventory
- Roles: all the commands in the **roles** section of the playbook
- Tasks: 'Check Cxn' and 'Show Config' **tasks** section of the playbook
- Module: **juniper_junos_command**

Note that it uses a variable called 'response' to print the output of the commands being launched in the tasks.

The following is an example of a playbook with multiple plays for routers and switches.

```
---
- name: Show route
  hosts: routers
  connection: local
  gather_facts: no
  tasks:
    - name: Show IP route information
      ios_command:
        authorize: yes
        lines:
          -  show ip route
      register: response
    - name: "Print result"
      debug:
        var: response

- name: Show VLAN
  hosts: switches
  connection: local
  gather_facts: no
  tasks:
    - name: Show VLAN number information
      ios_command:
        authorize: yes
        lines:
          -  show vlan
      register: response
    - name: "Print result"
      debug:
        var: response
```

The earlier described components are found as follows this playbook example.

- Play: the 'Show route' and 'Show VLAN' plays are each distinct
- Inventory: the route play has 'routers' whilst the 'VLAN' play has 'switches
- Roles: these are not used in this playbook
- Tasks: all the commands in the **tasks** sections of the playbook
- Module: **ios_command**

Note that it uses a variable called 'response' to print the output of the commands being launched in the tasks.

Inventory Setup

The Ansible inventory uses an INI file type of configuration as follows.

It can be saved with our without a file extension and can use any name with ASCII letters or numbers eg 'list' or 'list.txt'.

```
[db]
db1

[servers]
server1
192.168.1.1

[switches]
switch1
```

```
[firewalls]
firewall1
10.10.1.1
```

The square bracketed sections are user-defined. For example, note that the hosts: line in the earlier show playbook referenced firewalls. This is a section of the above inventory file would run on the firewall listed in this configuration section. The names shown in the inventory must be DNS-resolvable. Otherwise use IP addresses as shown below.

```
[db]
192.168.1.10
192.168.1.1

[servers]
192.168.1.7

[switches]
192.168.1.5

[firewalls]
192.168.1.8
10.10.1.1
```

Each of these sections can be referenced directly in the playbook to run it against them as shown below.

```
---
- name: SHOW VERSION AND SYSTEM COMMIT
  hosts: firewalls
```

Alternatively, all of the hosts in the inventory could be referenced in the playbook as shown below.

```
---
- name: SHOW VERSION AND SYSTEM COMMIT
  hosts: all
```

Variable Precedence

Variables can be defined in a number of places. So, there is the possibility that a variable is defined in different locations so Ansible needs a way of determine which particular value to use. This is done using its rules of variable precedence. These rules determine the variables based on the following order from least to most preferred variable.

1. Default
2. Group
3. Host
4. Play
5. Role
6. -e

So, variables set using the –e switch are preferred over all other variable settings.

Sequencing Playbooks in Ansible

Handlers

This is a special type of task than can be called by a playbook without having to be copied into the playbook each instance of its used. They are mostly used for service restarts as shown in the following example. It is called using the notify switch in a task. So, the following 'Install Nginx' task would run the 'Start Nginx' handler shown after the application is installed.

```
---
- hosts: all

  tasks:
    - name: Install Nginx
      apt: pkg=nginx state=installed
update_cache=true
      notify:
        - Start Nginx

  handlers:
    - name: Start Nginx
      service: name=nginx state=started
```

Nested Includes

It is possible to sequence playbooks by adding a link within a playbook to another. This is done using a nested include by setting the playbook to run with the include switch. An example of this is shown below. This will run the `servers.yml` playbook from the current playbook.

```
---
- hosts: all

  tasks:
    - name: Run commands on servers
      include: servers.yml
```

Using Conditions in Ansible

As stated previously, Ansible uses a declarative programming paradigm. But it can use conditional statements, for instance, to check for specific output before continuing to the next playbook task. These commands are shown in the following examples.

Waitfor Condition

The **waitfor** condition can be used to pause a playbook until the required output to a command is displayed.

Below is an example used to ensure that VLAN 500 appears in a Cisco switch interface's VLAN list before it saves the configuration.

```
---
- hosts: 192.168.1.1

  gather_facts: false
  connection: local

  tasks:
   - name: Check VLANs on Trunk
     ios_command:
       commands:
         - show run int vlan | i 500
       waitfor:
```

```yaml
        - result[0] contains 'switchport
access vlan.*,500,'

    - name: Save Config
      ios_config:
        authorize: yes
        save: yes
```

Ansible Vault

This is Ansibles in-built password security feature. It saves passwords in it using the following steps.

Add

```
---
vars_files:
  -   variables.yml

tasks:
  ios_command:
    command: ping {{ network_ip }}
```

The command to encrypt the variables file is as follows.

```
ansible vault encrypt variables.yml
```

This encrypts the file with a password whilst creating a key for it. Keep this key in a safe place.

The file contents would look similar to the following.

```
---
network_ip: 1.1.1.1
```

What Is Ansible Tower?

This is the server orchestration tool for Ansible. Note that playbooks cannot be written in Tower only managed. So why use it at all? Scale! Ansible Tower gives you a user-friendly interface in which to manage hundreds of playbooks via *Job Templates*. These can be daisy-chained, scheduled, copied and duplicated as well as secured by permissions so that only users with pre-assigned privileges can run them giving a level or control and organisation that cannot be attained by organising and running playbooks from the command line.

Installing Tower

Tower runs on either Ubuntu or Centos. The examples in this book are running on the Centos operating system.

Documentation states that 2GB RAM and 20GB disk space is enough but it is advisable to use higher amounts of resource.

Download the tarball from the installation path.

```
sudo curl -O -J
https://releases.ansible.com/ansible-
tower/setup/ansible-tower-setup-latest.tar.gz
```

Extract it.

```
tar xzf ansible-tower-setup-latest.tar.gz
```

```
cd ansible-tower-setup-latest
```

Check the newly created directory name using ls.

```
ls
```

Change the current directory path to the Ansible folder e.g. if the folder is called `ansible-tower-install-folder` run the following command.

```
cd ansible-tower-install-folder
```

Run setup.sh in this folder as root.

```
./setup.sh
```

The installation takes a few minutes so be patient whilst it installs all of the required components.

The installation guide at the time of writing can be found at the following location.

https://docs.ansible.com/ansible/latest/installation_guide/intro_installation.html

Navigating Ansible Tower

The menu at the top left of the Tower GUI has the following items as icons.

- Projects
- Inventories

- Templates
- Jobs

These are described further below.

A Note About Permissions

Each Tower resource will usually have a **PERMISSIONS** button at its top-level menu. This is where permissions can be set that control which users have access to the resource and what these users can actually do. These permissions include items such as roles and differ depending on the resource. But the will all typically have an Admin and a Read permission as a minimum.

Projects

This refers to the overall work that needs to be carried out by Tower to achieve a specific purpose e.g. build of a web server. It is the overall

Inventories

This is the list of devices that Tower will run the required playbooks on. These cannot be imported from files but can be dynamically generated using Inventory Scripts. Inventory Scripts can be written in Python to automatically add hosts to an inventory for Ansible Playbooks to run against, so devices can be added to the newly generated inventory depending on the configuration requirements.

Templates

These are the playbook templates that are used to carry out orchestration tasks.

The templates can then be used to carry out changes and user input can be requested using the *Survey* feature.

Access the current list of templates by clicking on its link.

If a new template is required, click on the green plus box to add it.

To edit a template in the list that appears click on the template's link.

Either way a window will appear showing the relevant fields that can be edited for the template. On editing all of the fields click the green save button to save.

Note that the template has the following buttons near the top that can be used to edit further information. The key fields are shown for each button.

- **Details**: name, inventory, project, playbook, credential
- **Permissions**: shows each user and its applicable roles
- **Notifications**:
- **Completed Jobs**: shows a list of completed jobs
- **Schedules**: on clicking green add button set start date, time, frequency, time zone, etc

Job Templates

These are the actual changes implemented using the playbooks saved as templates.

Note that Tower will not show playbooks that have issues in any of the playbook dropdowns.

Workflow Job Templates

These are a special type of job template can also be created to link multiple playbooks conditionally.

For example, if there were four playbooks required to implement a core switch change and they had to be launched in the following order.

1. access.yml
2. distro.yml
3. coreA.yml
4. coreB.yml

A workflow job template could be set up to link all of these playbooks in the order shown in the above list. This way, distro.yml would only run if access.yml ran successfully, coreA.yml would only run if distro.yml ran successfully and so on.

Job Templates and Workflow Job Templates are linked to Templates – think of the Template as the housing for Job and Workflow Job Templates.

Menu Settings

The menu at the top right of the Tower GUI has the following items as icons.

- Current User
- Settings
- My View
- View Documentation
- Logout

These are described as follows.

Credentials

This is where credentials can be added for use in logging into various resources required by Tower. For example, the login to a DSCM such as GitHub can be saved here.

Simply click on the green add button to add or click on a previously created credential to edit it and then edit the fields which will include but not be limited to the following.

- Name
- Description
- Organization
- Credential Type
- Username
- Password

Current User

Configure the currently logged in user's settings.

Settings

A lot of user time is spent in the Settings menu.

This menu has some or all of the following options depending on the current logged in user's privileges.

- Organizations
- Users
- Teams
- Credentials
- Management Jobs
- Inventory Scripts
- Notifications

- View Your Licence
- Configure Tower
- About Tower

These are described further below.

Organizations

This enables the management of jobs by department, company or other denominating factor.

All of the users and teams configured must belong to an organization.

Users

This is where the Tower users can be created and edited as well as have roles assigned to them.

Teams

Users can be put into relevant groups and have permissions applied to these groups here.

Credentials

Passwords, SSH keys and so on can be configured for the jobs and devices they are being run on with this setting.

Management Jobs

This where jobs can be tidied up and deleted to keep the server clean.

Inventory Scripts

Scripts can be created here to dynamically load devices from any source.

Notifications

Automated emails showing job status can be configured with this setting.

View Your Licence

Shows the current server's licencing information.

Configure Tower

Change the actual server configuration.

About Tower

Version information is shown in this view.

Roles

These are user-based roles synonymous with account privileges and access. They are not the same as the playbook roles described earlier in this book.

There are various roles types that can be used in Tower. These are summarised below.

- **User**: Admin, Use, Read
- **Team**: Admin, Member, Read

API

Tower has its own inbuilt application programming interface (API) that can be used to get or set its configuration using a URL.

Tower-cli

This is the command line tool that can be used to remotely execute jobs on a Tower server.

Installation

It can be installed using the pip command as follows.

```
pip install ansible-tower-cli
```

Configuration

The different variables that can be configured are shown below.

- TOWER_COLOR: color
- TOWER_FORMAT: format
- TOWER_HOST: host
- TOWER_PASSWORD: password
- TOWER_USERNAME: username
- TOWER_VERIFY_SSL: verify_ssl
- TOWER_VERBOSE: verbose

- **TOWER_DESCRIPTION_ON:** description_on
- **TOWER_CERTIFICATE:** certificate

View the current configuration by running the following command.

```
tower-cli config
```

This shows the values currently stored in the **/etc/tower/tower-cli.cfg** file. The location can differ per installation but this is the recommended location.

Configuration of any of the values shown can be done at the command line as follows. Note the fields being configured e.g. host, username, etc.

```
tower-cli config host tower.gridlockaz.com
tower-cli config username administrator
tower-cli config password securepassword
tower-cli config verbose CHECK
```

They can also be configured in the Tower config file as shown below.

```
host: tower.gridlockaz.com
username: administrator
password: securepassword
verbose: CHECK
```

Other commands are shown below

```
tower-cli user
tower-cli job
tower-cli group
tower-cli workflow schema WORKFLOW-NAME
```

My View

This shows your own account's view of the Ansible Tower dashboard. Check the documentation on how to configure this to suit.

View Documentation

This is the Ansible Tower documentation's repository.

Logout

Click on this link to log you out of the application.

Conclusion

That's it for now folks. Hopefully this has been a useful 'introduction' or 'reminder' of some key concepts and will continue to be useful to you as a serious networking professional. We are constantly striving to enhance the Big Little Book series so let us know if there are any topics you would like to see in future editions of this book. That's it for now, let us know if there's anything you would like added to the next edition of this book by sending an email to info@gridlockaz.com.

Thanks for reading and wishing you all the best in your career pursuits.

Take care.

U V Omos

www.ingramcontent.com/pod-product-compliance
Lightning Source LLC
Chambersburg PA
CBHW031232050326
40689CB00009B/1570